Juvenile

WITHDRAWN

INCREDIBLY DISGUSTING FOOD™

FAKE FOODS:
FRIED, FAST, AND PROCESSED
THE INCREDIBLY DISGUSTING STORY

Paula Johanson

New York

For the people at the Green Future discussion, making good choices

Published in 2011 by The Rosen Publishing Group, Inc.
29 East 21st Street, New York, NY 10010

Library of Congress Cataloging-in-Publication Data

Johanson, Paula.
Fake foods: fried, fast, and processed: the incredibly disgusting story / Paula Johanson.
   p. cm.—(Incredibly disgusting food)
Includes bibliographical references and index.
ISBN 978-1-4488-1269-1 (library binding)
ISBN 978-1-4488-2285-0 (pbk.)
ISBN 978-1-4488-2289-8 (6-pack)
1. Convenience foods—Health aspects—Juvenile literature. 2. Junk food—Health aspects—Juvenile literature. 3. Fried food—Health aspects—Juvenile literature. 4. Natural foods—Juvenile literature. I. Title.
TX370.J34 2011
642'.1—dc22

2010020534

Manufactured in the United States of America

CPSIA Compliance Information: Batch #W11YA: For further information, contact Rosen Publishing, New York, New York, at 1-800-237-9932.

CONTENTS

INTRODUCTION

When people are hungry, it's the most natural thing in the world to eat food. But are they eating real food? Unfortunately, a lot of what gets sold as food in grocery stores and restaurants is different from whole foods such as apples, milk, or carrots. Much of the food eaten in North America is fast food, or fried or processed to the point that it is no longer healthy, natural food. Nutritionist Marion Nestle calls it fake food and junk food, low in nutrition and high in salt, fat, sweeteners, and chemical preservatives and additives. "Food companies must stop marketing junk foods to kids," she says.

Processed food starts out with some food ingredients such as grains, vegetables, or dairy products. But these foods get chopped or milled, mixed with salt, sweeteners, mineral products, and preservatives, then cooked, and packaged in plastic. They're so thoroughly processed that Michael Pollan, author of *Food Rules*, calls them "food-like

products." These are factory products, processed as thoroughly as a can of paint or a music player.

Fried foods can start out with fresh, healthy ingredients, such as eggs or potatoes. But if they're fried on a griddle, most restaurants and food manufacturers use a lot of oil. That fat can be beef tallow or pork lard, or cottonseed oil turned into trans fats. Foods that are deep-fried in a vat of hot fat absorb much of that fat. Fat in fried food puts a lot of extra calories into human bodies, making it easy for people who eat a lot of fried food to become overweight or obese and have health problems.

Fast food is usually processed and often fried. It's quick and convenient to grab some fast food. But these foods often have sweeteners added, such as high fructose corn syrup, which means people will feel hungry again

Restaurants will soon serve more healthy fried foods, as more cities and states are banning the use of trans fats in restaurants and bakeries. Doughnuts, chicken, or fries will still taste good!

soon after eating them. In addition, they're often packaged in wrappers with phthalates, chemicals that may cause changes to human nerves and hormones.

Thinking about fake food—fast, fried, and processed—is pretty disgusting. It's enough to make anyone lose his or her appetite. But there are plenty of options for foods that are not disgusting. There are real foods that are just as quick to pick up and eat as fast food, but that give human bodies healthy fuel for good health. There are snacks and even lightly fried foods that are tasty and tempting and that don't have corn syrup or the heavy sludge of trans fats. Real food can be processed at home, and in restaurants, too. Even food processed in factories can be made healthy instead of just easy to deliver and sell.

It may seem like there's no point in taking all that trouble to use healthy foods and good ingredients for something as ordinary as meals. Fake food may not seem like a problem until people look closer at what they're eating and how it affects them. There are some unhappy surprises to learn about many popular fake foods. People's bodies react to these foods in ways that are really disgusting.

MAKING FAKE FOODS

Fake foods don't grow on trees. People make fake foods. People can learn to make them healthier than they are usually made. Some of the most popular fast foods are hamburgers, french fries, tacos, soda pop, breakfast cereal, fried chicken, and pizza. Many of these fast foods are processed, as are fried foods, too. The ways that processed foods, fried foods, and fast foods are made can be astonishing. There are a lot of questions worth asking before eating something. What's in this food? Where did it come from? Who made it?

How Hamburgers Stack Up

Hamburgers can be real food, made from lean meat, organically raised. A good hamburger is served on a whole grain bun with trimmings such as romaine lettuce or spinach and slices of tomato and onion. It takes several minutes to cook a hamburger and serve it on a plate with freshly sliced trimmings.

Most fast-food hamburgers are made from high-fat meat that is ground up with bits of tough meat and gristle. Most American fast-food hamburger patties are made in one of only fifteen large slaughterhouses. The meat inspectors are kept so busy that they have time to check only one side of a carcass for tumors and injuries. The biggest hamburger restaurant chains in the United States don't buy young steers for meat. They pay less for old dairy cows that have been pregnant all their lives and have been given growth hormones to increase milk production. The leftover bits of meat from the carcasses of hundreds of animals are ground together and shaped into patties that are frozen in a factory.

Does your local restaurant use good ground meat and no added trans fats on the griddle? Clean hands in a clean restaurant means workers can be proud of making good burgers.

Most of these patties are fried in grease on a griddle and kept warm until a kitchen worker places the patties on buns made from bleached white flour. A squirt of sweet ketchup and a sprinkle of mechanically diced onion are no substitutes for fresh toppings. A few shreds of iceberg lettuce have almost no nutritional value. The fast-food version of a hamburger may be easy to buy, but it's not much like real food.

Po-TAY-toh, Po-TAH-toh

French fries for fast-food restaurants aren't cut from fresh potatoes like they are when people prepare them at home. Commercially made french fries are slightly boiled, frozen, and then packaged to be trucked hundreds of miles. In some factories, french fries are shaped out of

This factory turns tons of fresh potatoes into industrial food products. Potatoes are cut into hash browns and french fries, boiled, salted, frozen, and shipped for hundreds of miles.

cooked, mashed potatoes. Restaurants cook the frozen fries in vats of hot fat—animal or vegetable oil. Most restaurants change the oil every week or two. The used fat is sometimes recycled to make lipstick—not a pretty thought.

A popular international restaurant chain used to use a combination of beef tallow and pork lard to cook french fries. When customers learned that fact, many communities were outraged and disgusted. The use of pork products is forbidden for both Jewish kosher food traditions and for Muslim halal food traditions because pigs are considered unclean. Moreover, people who eat kosher do not mix meat and milk in the same meal. In Hindu traditions, beef products are not eaten because cows are regarded as holy animals. Vegetarian customers insisted that vegetable oil should be used instead of animal products. The restaurant chain found that its french fries tasted different when they did not use beef fat, so in many countries the chain adds hydrolyzed beef flavor to the potatoes. This restaurant chain is now trying to please some of its customers in some countries. But food laws don't make restaurants print this specific information on their menus.

Lukewarm Food Laws

Food laws are ways that governments try to ensure that food is handled and prepared safely in restaurants and stores. Germs that cause foodborne illness grow when food is held at the incorrect temperature. It can be hot food that's kept barely warm before being served or cold food that's kept at room temperature instead of in a cold refrigerator.

What's Convenient About Convenience Foods?

Fake foods are convenient for being sold to customers. That's all. A big business finds it very convenient to make, store, sell, and deliver food products as if they were plain, identical things like bricks. But these fake foods aren't "convenient" for what human bodies need in terms of nutrition. Fresh food has a variety of benefits for people's bodies that processed food often lacks. There are vitamins and minerals for nutrition and tastes and textures for enjoyment. Real food is actually very convenient. It gives people the calories they need for fuel, neatly delivered with many kinds of nutrients and fibers to keep individuals healthy.

Tacos are a good example of fast food that needs to be kept at the proper temperature. Fried ground meat must be kept hot until the taco is put together. The trimmings of chopped lettuce, sliced tomatoes, and grated cheese must be kept cold. The spicy sauce could be kept cold or hot, not room temperature. Workers must have clean hands or clean gloves, and the kitchen must be kept clean. It can be a challenge to keep each food at the correct temperature until it is served.

More than two-thirds of restaurants "had at least one high-risk food safety violation," according to a survey conducted by the Center for Science in the Public Interest (CSPI) in twenty U.S. cities. "The most critical violations cited included: 26 percent of restaurants were cited for contaminated food contact surfaces, 22 percent of restaurants were cited for improper holding temperatures, 16 percent of restaurants were cited for inadequate hand washing by employees, 13 percent of restaurants were cited for rodent/insect activity." It's not enough to have laws about clean hands, clean kitchens, and the appropriate temperature to store and serve food. Restaurants must be inspected regularly and made to do the right thing.

Sugar is part of the good taste of an apple or a beet. It's easy to eat too much sweetener processed from corn or cane or beets and added to processed food.

Pop Quiz

Question: How much sugar is in a soft drink? Answer: More than you might think, and probably more than you can believe. Most people who make a sweet drink such as iced tea at home add one or two spoonfuls of sugar. But cans of iced tea contain 7 or more teaspoons (34.5 milliliters) of sugar. The average can of soda pop has up to 12 teaspoons (59.2 ml) of sugar. Drinking just one can of a soft drink each day adds a lot of empty calories to a person's diet without adding the minerals that are in milk or the vitamins and fiber in pulpy orange juice. Soda pop makes a bad snack if consumed too frequently. What's worse is that more than a third of all the cola drinks sold in North America are drunk for breakfast and lunch, instead of milk or juice.

A Quick Breakfast

A bowl of cereal is a simple, fast breakfast. But it's a good idea to read the ingredients listed on a box of cereal before deciding whether it is real breakfast food.

Many packaged cereals have two or three times as much sugar and salt as people would add to oatmeal, porridge, or granola they make at home. Artificial food colors and flavors are added to some cereals to make them interesting to children. Packaged cereal is often made from bleached white flour, not whole wheat flour. Corn flour, salt, and sweeteners made from corn are usually added. There are also chemical preservatives added to most packaged cereals, which aren't needed for bags of dry oatmeal, cornmeal, or cracked grain porridge.

A few packaged cereals are made with whole grains, including fiber in wheat bran and healthy oils in wheat germ. But look carefully at the rest of the ingredients! At least seven popular whole grain cereals are promoted as being "fortified" with minerals. They get those minerals by adding trisodium phosphate (TSP). The chemical TSP is an industrial cleaner that takes oil stains off driveways and is used in toilet bowl cleaner and laundry and dishwasher detergents.

You can see tasty spices on this fried chicken! But you can't see added salt and sweeteners, or tell if the chickens were crowded in cages or raised on cruelty-free farms.

Take It Away!

Millions of people who never bake pizza or deep-fry pieces of chicken are glad to be able to go to take-out restaurants. These take-out fake foods look like food someone might cook at home. But look carefully! Take-out restaurants use twice as much salt, or more, as anyone does at home. Corn syrup is added to pizza sauce and to batter for fried chicken. Only a few privately owned restaurants have recipes with little or no salt and sweetener added.

No one would eat take-out chicken or pizza if they saw how animals were raised to make chicken pieces or pepperoni sausage for pizza. On factory farms, pigs are crowded into pens. Their tails are cut off so they don't bite each other from boredom. Some pigs are kept in small cages all their lives. On factory farms, chickens are crowded into barns and sometimes stacked in cages. Chickens raised for meat grow so quickly that their legs often become crippled from trying to hold up their big, meaty chests. Factory farm animals' food grain is mixed with chopped animal guts and dried blood from slaughterhouses.

Nutritionist Marion Nestle collected research showing that the suffering and bad diets of animals raised on factory farms cause many health problems and allergies in humans when they consume the meat, milk, and eggs from these creatures. "How are we treating the animals we eat while they're alive," asks Michael Pollan, "and then how humanely are we 'dispatching' them?"

2···· HOW FAKE FOODS AFFECT YOUR BODY

Human bodies need more from food than just calories for fuel. A variety of nutrients are needed on a daily basis. Children and young adults have differing needs because they are still growing. Eating fake foods has negative effects on people's bodies, making it difficult to build strong muscles or get better from a head cold because the fake foods often lack vitamins, minerals, and protein. Even day to day, the bad effects of eating fake foods can be noticed. Many people find they develop more pimples and boils, for example. Going to the bathroom can become complicated—too much salt and sugar makes people dehydrated and the fake foods lack fiber. It's easy to end up with constipation or diarrhea.

The effect of even one meal can be considerable. People training for athletic events often load up on complex carbohydrates the day before the event so that they will have a lot of energy available.

But fake foods can be full of sugar and are no substitute for whole grain pasta with good homemade sauce.

Give Me Some Sugar!

There are some kinds of sugar that are naturally in fruits and vegetables. Many fake foods have processed sugars added instead of natural juice sweeteners. Fake foods don't have all of the vegetable fiber that makes the sugar take longer to be digested. Sweet fake food, such as candy or soda pop, lets that sugar be digested quickly. A person gets a lot of sugar in the blood right away, and the pancreas makes enzymes to help use up that sugar quickly. Blood sugar can rise quickly and give a lot of energy, then the blood sugar gets used up and falls just as quickly, and the person feels tired and weak.

Fake food products such as soda pop or cakes have a lot of high fructose corn syrup added. These fake foods cause rebound hunger—an hour or so after eating, the person is hungry again. This rebound hunger increases a person's chance of becoming overweight or obese because people will end up eating more. It affects a person's mind,

Fruity candies just *look* like fake berries and licorice. Try real fruits or licorice root. Apples naturally have the tart taste of malic acid that's added to sour candy.

too. Studies have shown that alertness and learning potential in school drops after the first hour for students who have soft drinks and sugary cereal for breakfast.

Deep Fat Is Deep Trouble

That uncomfortable feeling after eating greasy fried food isn't just from being too full. It's the gallbladder trying to make extra digestive fluids even though gallstones are in the way. Stressed gallbladders form lumps called gallstones, which can restrict or block the duct connecting the liver, gall-bladder, and pancreas to the upper part of the intestine. Most American adults eat so much fat that many of them have small gall-stones and don't know it. So do many overweight children.

This artwork shows a gallbladder, cut away to view gallstones forming. To lower your risk of getting gall-stones, avoid eating greasy and high cholesterol foods containing saturated and trans fats.

Don't Fake It!

Because eating too much fat is bad for people's health, doctors have been researching alternatives. One invention is fake fat or fat substitute. The long chain molecules that make up the fat have been changed so that the altered fat cannot be digested. It sounds like a good idea to invent fake fat that can be used to make potato chips or other snack foods. When someone eats these chips, the fake fat doesn't get absorbed into the bloodstream.

Yet, inside a person's colon, fake fat isn't such a good idea after all. The fake fat turns into lumps that don't move easily along the colon. That makes it hard to have a bowel movement. People can get cramps and become con-stipated. In addition, as the solid wastes get packed into the lower colon, the fake fat can also make liquid waste that leaks around the lump. Read the labels on snack foods carefully to see if fake fat is an ingredient—a warning label about "anal leakage" means "stained underwear."

Restaurants Are Part of the Problem

People who work in restaurants are food professionals, and customers depend on them. "On a typical day, 44 percent of American adults eat at a restaurant. Unfortunately, the rate of foodborne illness from restaurant food is disturbingly high," wrote Sarah Klein and Caroline Smith DeWaal in *Dirty Dining*, a report for the CSPI. "Data from 1990 through 2006 indicate that 41 percent of all foodborne illness outbreaks can be traced to restaurant food, compared to 22 percent from private homes."

How Much Fake Food Is Too Much?

Some people think they can get away with eating fake foods for years. Others feel that it's wrong to eat anything that they didn't grow in their own farms and gardens. For most people the truth lies somewhere in between these two extremes. People have always eaten a variety of whole foods. Some people feel that eating a little fake food is just part of that variety. There are fake foods that seem to take years to cause chronic health problems in most people. Other fake foods take a day, a month, or even a year to negatively affect people. Choosing whether to eat fake food is not a matter of confidence or prejudice. It's a matter of letting your body decide.

Foodborne illness can be an *E. coli* infection, which causes a couple of uncomfortable days of nausea, vomiting, and diarrhea. The more severe form known as *E. coli* 0157:H7 causes bloody diarrhea and may cause life-threatening kidney failure. Other foodborne illnesses are caused by germs such as *Norovirus*, *Salmonella*, *Clostridium*, and *C. botulinum*. *Norovirus* infections are also known as Norwalk viruses (after Norwalk, Ohio, where an outbreak of the virus was first identified in 1972). Nurses commonly joke that patients who have food poisoning are "Norwalking" when they run to a toilet while holding a bucket for vomiting.

How can restaurant food make people sick? In *Dirty Dining*, Klein and DeWaal quote a report from the U.S. Food and Drug Administration (FDA) that says 75 percent of restaurant employees do not wash their hands or don't do so satisfactorily. They also note that "There can be as many germs beneath a ring, for example, as there are people in Europe."

Some kinds of foodborne illness such as listeriosis, caused by *Listeria* bacteria, can spread from germs on contaminated machines and surfaces in factories, where a lot of food is cut and packaged. *Listeria* is usually found in the soil and water. Animals eat or drink food or water that is tainted with *Listeria*. People who eat the meat from these animals get very ill if the meat hasn't been cooked at a high enough temperature to kill the bacteria. Milk is pasteurized to kill bacteria. But people's hands are a more common problem for foodborne illnesses. "Three pathogens come primarily from infected workers: Hepatitis A virus, and *Shigella* and *Staphylococcus aureus* bacteria," Klein and DeWaal point out. "Hepatitis A and *Shigella* are carried in human fecal matter [bodily waste]. The illnesses they cause can be prevented by proper hand washing." This is a problem that people can solve.

It's normal for people to have some *Escherichia coli* bacteria in their intestines. But this variety of *E. coli*, shown here stained purple and magnified 1,500 times, makes toxins that can be fatal.

All Wrapped Up

Fast food is usually wrapped in disposable wrappers. These wrappers are easy to throw away, but unlike paper, they take a long time to break down on the ground or in the garbage. The soft plastic of the wrappers is full of chemicals such as phthalates, which make food taste like plastic. These chemicals have effects similar to hormones on people's bodies. Studies are still being done to learn how quickly the chemicals, which can alter people's mood and overall health, take effect. These chemicals work with other factors to make puberty occur earlier in some children—sometimes in kids as young as six or seven years old. Another effect of these hormonelike chemicals is to cause swollen breasts in some teenage males.

MYTHS AND FACTS

Myth: Fresh foods are expensive.

Fact: Processed foods cost more per bite than fresh foods. It is also expensive to treat the heart attacks, diabetes, strokes, cancer, and depression that fake foods can cause.

Myth: Take-out fried chicken is just like the chicken that grandmother used to make.

Fact: Nobody's grandmother ever raised her chickens crowded in wire cages stacked in a barn. Nobody's grandmother ever put hydrolyzed soy protein or beef flavor in the batter before deep-frying chicken pieces in genetically modified canola oil.

Myth: Ads don't really make me buy any food.

Fact: Most young people buy processed food products that are advertised on television and in stores.

3

HEALTH CHANGES: NOW AND LATER

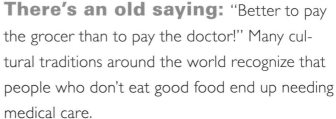

There's an old saying: "Better to pay the grocer than to pay the doctor!" Many cultural traditions around the world recognize that people who don't eat good food end up needing medical care.

Health is something to consider not only just one person at a time, but also as a group or society. Food writer Michael Pollan, in his book *Food Rules: An Eater's Manual*, writes that "Populations that eat a so-called Western diet—generally defined as a diet consisting of lots of processed foods … invariably suffer from high rates of the so-called Western diseases: obesity, type 2 diabetes, cardiovascular disease and cancer." In looking at the lives of thousands of people, doctors are learning how to diagnose what makes whole societies healthy or ill.

The Bottom Line

Eating mostly fast food and processed food can cause more than just a day or two of diarrhea or

constipation. Long-term constipation and diarrhea lead to the
formation of hemorrhoids
and contribute to diver-
ticulosis, diverticulitis,
and colon cancer.
These are chronic
conditions that
cause a lot of pain.
These conditions
also make people feel
uncomfortable and
embarrassed.

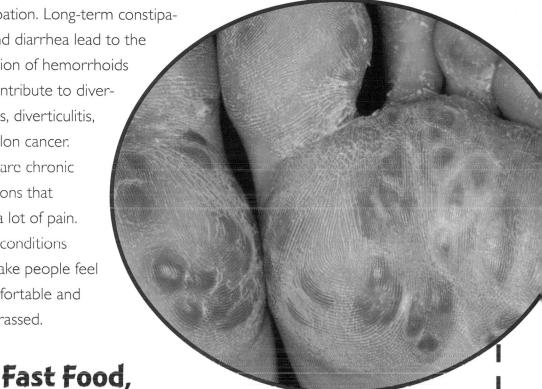

Fast Food, Lasting Effects

Indigestion or food poisoning can mean more than just an uncomfortable
day or two with an aching stomach. A single fast-food meal can have life-long
aftereffects.

Food poisoning infections with *Salmonella* or other germs can cause
long-term complications, such as reactive arthritis, also known as Reiter's
syndrome. This illness causes
inflamed joints, eyes, and
urethras. Many doctors
remember this illness by the

Food poisoning can cause more than just vomiting and
diarrhea. People who develop Reiter's syndrome suffer
from inflamed joints, eyes, and urethras, and hard
nodules on their skin, like those on this person's feet.

verse "The patient can't see, can't pee, can't bend the knee." The deep, aching pain is often severe. Some patients need several shots of morphine each day for weeks while in the hospital. Some patients are still too sore a year later to turn a key in a car's ignition or too stiff to put on a coat without assistance. Bill Marler, a lawyer who works to help people who have been harmed by foodborne illnesses, writes that "General sanitary techniques of hand washing and clean drinking water have decreased the incidence of these infections in industrialized countries, but they are still very prevalent [widespread] in less developed countries and the third world." Symptoms of severe arthritis can be permanent.

Digesting a single fatty fried meal can cause lasting problems. A gallstone that previously caused no warning symptoms may suddenly block the duct and cause permanent damage to both the gallbladder and the pancreas. Blocked ducts can lead to appendicitis, pancreas failure, and diabetes. The pain of an inflamed pancreas is caused by the enzymes leaking out, which digest some of the body's own tissues. People who ignore that pain aren't tough and brave; they're risking surgery, chronic pain, and diabetes. People can end up needing to take pills or give themselves a shot every day for the rest of their lives because the pancreas no longer makes enough enzymes or insulin.

Fake foods can be especially risky for people who have allergies. Fast-food restaurants often mix up food orders and ingredients even at the best of times. For someone with an allergy, it's hard to know for sure if any restaurant has prepared food that is safe to eat. In addition, most processed food contains the common allergens corn, soybeans, wheat, and milk products. Factories that process nuts and peanuts for a specific food can put crumbs into other products when they use the same machinery for all of the items. People who have food allergies have to read labels very carefully. Some people have hives and stomachaches for weeks after eating a meal with the wrong food in it. But people who are allergic to nuts or seafood can die just from licking a dirty spoon or taking one bite of food with peanut crumbs in it.

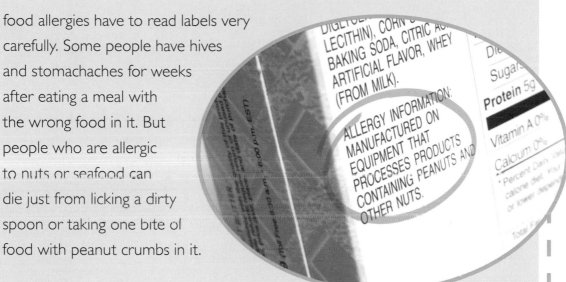

What Causes Cancer?

Usually, there's no single reason why someone gets cancer. The diet a person eats is only one factor among many. Luckily, diet is something people can change.

The Western diet includes a lot of processed, fried, and fast food. "Virtually all of the obesity and type 2 diabetes, 80 percent of the cardio-vascular disease, and more than a third of all cancers can be linked to this diet," writes Michael Pollan. "In countries where people eat a pound or more of vegetables and fruits a day, the rate of cancer is half what it is in the United States." Doctors aren't sure of precisely what in the Western diet is causing cancer and other illnesses. But it's pretty clear that there are fewer cases of cancer in people who eat some fruits and vegetables every day instead of fake foods.

What food products can you eat even if you have a peanut allergy? Read labels! Labels show information about ingredients in processed food and how food products are made.

- Whose Fault Is Bad Health? - -

Accidents do happen, and people accept that. Some sports are risky, and people accept that. But there's no reason to accept bad health that comes from eating fake foods instead of real food. It's easy to say that a person who jumps off a roof onto a homemade trampoline is putting his or her life in danger. But whose fault is it when some people with diabetes go blind and others lose both feet to gangrene? "The cost of diabetes in the U.S. alone is $700 [each year] for every man, woman and child," writes scholar and activist Raj Patel. "For people of color, diet-related disease is incredibly important—one in two children of color born in 2000 will develop diabetes."

Brain Food

"If you've ever wondered why fatty food tastes so good, there are reasons why. Your brain and body need fat to function well," says psychologist Bruce Mansbridge. "The tissues of your brain and nerves are about 60 percent fat by weight." Eating fake foods labeled "fat-free" does no good for a brain hungry for the oils in fish and vegetables.

Processed food is linked by writer Gracelyn Guyol, who was diagnosed with a mild bipolar disorder, to rising rates of depression, anxiety disorders, and even epilepsy. Part of the problem is chemical preservatives in processed food, and part is bad fats. A packaged snack cake won't rot for a year on a store shelf, but in a human body the trans fats in the cake will clog blood vessels. Certain kinds of fats are very good for brain and nerve functions, but these good fats are absent from most processed and fast foods. "The

fat and oils in fish are particularly good for growing and maintaining a healthy brain," according
to Mansbridge. "Studies have proved the
benefits of including fish oils in the diet of
people being treated for depression."

Overweight But Malnourished

People's bodies need more from food
than just a full stomach. They need many
kinds of nutrition from a variety of foods. Many
North Americans are now being diagnosed with chronic
diseases caused by malnutrition: kwashiorkor, pellagra, and beriberi. Some
people whose teeth fall out from scurvy are overweight or obese—they eat
plenty of calories but not enough vitamins and minerals.

"Food companies will make and market any product that sells, regardless of
its nutritional value or its effect on health," writes nutritionist Marion Nestle.
"In this regard, food companies hardly differ from cigarette companies."

This coronary artery should be a hollow tube, but the white layer
of plaque makes it too narrow for much blood to flow through.
Pieces of plaque block arteries, causing heart attacks or strokes.

4

EATING REAL FOOD

There are plenty of reasons for eating real food instead of fake food. Start with good tastes and interesting textures. Try new recipes and new small restaurants. Good health feels better than being bloated or tired. Those are good reasons to make a salad for lunch!

That's not to say that someone who eats no fruits or vegetables should start by eating a pound and a half the first day of a new diet. That could be really uncomfortable. But eating one apple the first day is a good start. Every week or so, try replacing one serving of fast food or candy each day with a handful of vegetables or a piece of fruit. In a month or two, that adds up to a lot of fresh food eaten every day.

Real Foods for Breakfast

There are more choices for breakfast than a box of sweetened cereal, processed into brightly colored shapes. "Don't eat cereal that changes the color of the milk," advises Michael Pollan. Many kinds of homemade cereal using rolled oats and wheat germ, for example, take only a minute to make, using a microwave or a kettle of boiling water. Fresh, dried, or frozen fruit is a great addition to plain yogurt. A breakfast wrap can be made with a whole wheat tortilla wrapped around scrambled eggs and mushrooms or diced peppers.

Making Take-Out Lunches

Lunch is a good time to start replacing fake foods with real food. Lunch food doesn't have to be bought sealed in wrappers. It's not hard to make sandwiches with whole grain bread. Cheese, boiled eggs, and raw vegetables are easy to slice up. A casserole can be cut into individual portions and sealed in bowls with lids. That's also a good way to carry salads, with a separate container for dressing. A thermos is a good way to carry homemade soup and keep it hot. There are bakeries that make

> Breakfast doesn't have to be fake food full of salt or sweeteners. Homemade granola with yogurt tastes great. So do oatmeal and whole grain cereals, especially with real fruit, milk, or juice.

Some of the best-tasting snacks are real foods that have no ads, no labels, and no wrappers. Your friends might like eating popcorn that has been prepared in a hot-air popper as much as you do.

muffins and cookies as good as homemade ones, with half the sugar, fats, and salt of most commercial baked goods.

Snack Food Can Be Real Food

There are plenty of alternatives to a candy bar. Many so-called chocolate bars are actually made mostly of sugar or sweeteners manufactured from corn. Candy bars are less than 12 percent chocolate. These bars don't melt on a warm day because carnauba wax is added. People who want to eat something sweet might want an orange, not a piece of shoe polish mixed with corn syrup. But many stores don't sell fresh fruit, only processed sweets sealed in plastic wrappers.

- - Ask Questions About Ads - - ⌐

Ads for food are usually ads for fast food and processed food products. Ask yourself: What is being sold in this ad—real food or an attitude? When have you ever seen an ad for a strawberry? There's no need to make up a peppy song for strawberries or put them in a pretty wrapper. Strawberries aren't labeled as having 10 percent of a daily recommended vitamin. Real food doesn't need decorations or high-pressure advertising.

It's easy to carry a pear or an orange for a snack. Other kinds of fruit such as peaches, bananas, or grapes may need to be carried in a little container. Vegetables such as beans and broccoli make tasty snacks, too. There are tidy little bags of peeled carrots sold in grocery stores. It's fun to taste different fruits and vegetables as they become ripe each season.

There are salty alternatives to potato chips. One choice is natural popcorn. It's real food when people buy a bag of kernels to pop. But when popcorn kernels for microwaving are packaged with "buttery" flavoring, that greasy additive isn't butter. It's made of artificial ingredients that cause factory workers to get rashes and lung diseases, and even die. The National Institute for Occupational Safety and Health (NIOSH) links exposure to dicetyl in the "buttery" flavoring to lung disease in popcorn factory workers. The added salt is twice or three times as much as most people add to a serving of popcorn.

A bag of plain kernels is much less expensive than packaged microwave bags of popcorn. Popcorn kernels can be microwaved in a paper bag or popped in a hot-air popper. Plain popcorn tastes good, or drizzle on a little melted butter (one spoonful) on a big bowl. Adding a sprinkle of garlic powder or other spices or even a tablespoon of ground Parmesan cheese will make it taste great! Or maybe for a birthday party, use a little melted butter and a bit of maple syrup to make sweet popcorn balls to share.

Dinners That Satisfy

A fast dinner doesn't have to be take-out chicken or fast-food hamburgers, not when salads and roasts are easy to make. A good way to start is by replacing one fake food dinner each week with real food. Making ordinary dinners out of real foods gets easier and easier with practice. There are cookbooks in libraries. Ask friends and relatives how to make special cultural dishes—some people enjoy sharing recipes and cooking techniques.

A fun way to enjoy a number of different dishes is to hold a potluck dinner. When each person brings a different dish, no one works too hard to prepare the entire meal. A similar idea works for a pizza party. Instead of having pizza delivered, start with homemade crusts or a pack of whole wheat tortillas. Add some tomato sauce and grate some cheese. Let everyone top the pizzas with peppers, tomatoes, mushrooms, or their own favorites. Look for meat from animals raised on local small farms.

Homegrown and Farm-Fresh

A good alternative to purchasing fake food shipped from factories is to buy fresh food grown on local farms. The Slow Food movement and the 100-Mile Diet both encourage people to enjoy seasonal foods that are locally grown. Farmers' markets bring fresh produce to customers in cities and towns. When enough customers ask for local food, grocery stores can carry and label local produce, and restaurants can buy supplies from local farmers. "For 300 years, this country's family farmers produced more than enough . . . for American consumers," writes Robert F. Kennedy Jr. in his book *Crimes Against Nature*. "Study after study shows that these small operations are far more efficient than the giant farm factories. But agribusiness has used its political and financial clout to eliminate agricultural markets, seize federal subsidies, and flout environmental laws to gain competitive advantage."

Who's in Charge?

Parents feel responsible for choosing good food for their children's growing bodies. As young people grow up, they each become responsible for what they eat. It's hard to make good choices, though, when the nearest store sells three kinds of crispy pork rinds but no peanut butter, for example.

Food laws can be passed to help people become less dependent on food choices made by businesses and organizations. The state of California passed laws in 2008 requiring that public schools not sell soft drinks or high-calorie, high-fat foods during school hours. In 2006, New York City banned the use of trans fats in restaurants, and other

Vegetables and fruits taste so good when they're locally grown and fresh-picked. Farmers' markets give small businesses with good products a chance to reach customers in towns and cities.

cities such as Boston and Chicago are considering similar laws. Santa Clara County in Silicon Valley, California, proposed a local law in 2010 to prevent restaurants from giving toys with children's meals that don't meet U.S. government nutrition rules for limits on salt, fat, and sugar. Ken Yeager of Santa Clara says the law "helps parents make the choices they want for their children without toys and other freebies luring them towards foods that fail to meet basic nutritional standards."

Every dollar spent on food supports business. "The average American family spends almost half of all its food dollars on restaurant food, and each American consumer eats out at least five times a week," wrote Klein and DeWaal in *Dirty Dining*. It's up to everyone to decide if they want to eat real food from farmers or fake food from factory corporations. Local restaurant and store owners make real food available when their customers insist on real food choices, not just fake foods. Even corporations make their factory food more like real food—better ingredients, better processing, less packaging—when consumers insist on eating real food.

The owner and chef of an acclaimed restaurant in New York City uses soybean oil without trans fats to fry food. In 2006, New York became the first U.S. city to ban the use of trans fats in restaurants.

TEN GREAT QUESTIONS TO ASK A NUTRITIONIST

1: How many fresh fruits and vegetables should I eat every day?

2: Are there any kinds of food that I should never eat?

3: How can people tell if they have any food allergies?

4: Are there any preservatives or other chemicals used in fast foods or processed foods that I need to be worried about eating?

5: How can I use a fast-food restaurant's nutritional information as a guide to choosing the right foods?

6: Where can I get some recipes for food that tastes good?

7: Is there a local cooking club or class where I can learn to cook food that is healthy?

8: Is there a store or farmers' market nearby where I can buy fresh fruits and vegetables?

9: What are some healthy choices for hot and cold drinks?

10: What are the best ways to limit the amount of trans fats in my diet?

GLOSSARY

allergens Substances (usually proteins) that cause an allergic response by the immune system, such as hives, swelling, stomachaches, hyperactivity, rashes, or problems breathing.

beriberi A disease caused by lack of thiamine (vitamin B_1) and characterized by inflammation of nerves, heart disease, and swelling of the body's organs.

bipolar disorder A condition that is characterized by alternating depressed and manic states.

calories The energy your body gets from food. Carbohydrates and proteins have four calories per gram; fat has nine calories per gram.

carnauba wax A wax obtained from the leaves of the carnauba palm and commonly used in car wax, shoe polish, wood finishing, and low-priced candy bars.

chronic Always present, as in a long-lasting disease or condition.

dicetyl A chemical used in artificial butter flavoring, snacks, and bakery products. Tests conducted at the National Institute for Occupational Safety and Health (an agency of the Centers for Disease Control and Prevention) using dicetyl showed lung damage in laboratory rats.

diverticula Small pouches in the colon that bulge out through the colon or intestines. When food gets trapped in the pouches, it causes inflammation (diverticulitis).

E. coli A bacterium, *Escherichia coli*, that lives in human and animal intestines. Usually infection causes mild diarrhea or no symptoms.

fiber Bulky cells in plant and animal tissue that can absorb water or give a tough texture to food, promoting good digestion.

halal Foods that are permitted under Islamic law.

hemorrhoids Areas of the rectum that become inflamed and swollen.

hydrolyze To break down into components, as in hydrolyzed protein that has been broken down into amino acids. Hydrolyzed protein is often used to improve the flavor of foods and contains monosodium glutamate, a food additive.

kosher Foods that are sanctioned by Jewish law.

kwashiorkor An often fatal illness that is caused by lack of protein in the diet.

monosodium glutamate A food additive that causes food allergies and nervous system symptoms; it is used in processed foods and as a spice in some Asian cooking.

100-Mile Diet Eating food grown within 100 miles (161 kilometers) of one's home; this diet is promoted in a book by James MacKinnon and Alisa Smith.

pasteurize A heat treatment invented by Louis Pasteur in 1864 to kill germs in milk or other foods without influencing the flavor or quality of the food.

pellagra A disease that occurs when someone does not get enough niacin (a B complex vitamin) in his or her diet; victims can suffer skin sores, diarrhea, and mental confusion.

phthalates Chemicals, used to soften plastic, that have hormonelike effects on human and animal bodies.

Salmonella A bacterium transferred from animals to humans through food that is not cooked thoroughly. It causes vomiting and severe diarrhea.

Slow Food movement An international nonprofit ecological and gastronomic organization promoting local food traditions; founded by Carlo Petrini in 1989.

trans fats Oils that have been hydrogenated (have had hydrogen gas bubbled through them) to make them hard at room temperature by adding hydrogen atoms to the long molecule of fat. Trans fats have been linked to high blood sugar, high amounts of bad cholesterol and low amounts of good cholesterol in the blood, and to obesity and cardiovascular disease.

vitamins Nutrients essential to the human body for health. They are found in fruits, vegetables, grains, fungi, meats, and dairy foods.

FOR MORE INFORMATION

American Dietetic Association (ADA)

120 South Riverside Plaza, Suite 2000

Chicago, IL 60606-6995

(800) 877-1600

Web site: http://www.eatright.org

The ADA is an association of food and nutrition experts who help people make food choices to promote health and reduce obesity.

Canadian Council of Food and Nutrition

2810 Matheson Boulevard East, First Floor

Mississauga, ON L4W 4X7

Canada

(905) 625-5746

Web site: http://www.nin.ca

Health professionals in this Canadian organization teach nutrition and food issues to the public.

Canadian Institutes of Health Research (CIHR)

160 Elgin Street, Ninth Floor

Address Locator 4809A

Ottawa, ON K1A 0W9

Canada

(888) 603-4178

Web site: http://www.cihr-irsc.gc.ca

The CIHR collaborates on research projects with industry, health charities, and government departments.

Center for Science in the Public Interest (CSPI)

1875 Connecticut Avenue NW, Suite 300

Washington, DC 20009

Web site: http://www.cspinet.org

CSPI is a nonprofit health-advocacy organization supported by subscribers to its Nutrition Action Healthletter, with no industry or government funding. CSPI led efforts to pass the law requiring nutrition labeling and has publicized the nutritional content of many popular restaurant foods.

MyPyramid.gov

USDA Center for Nutrition Policy and Promotion

3101 Park Center Drive, Room 1034

Alexandria, VA 22302-1594

(888) 779-7264

Web site: http://www.mypyramid.gov

This USDA Web site lets visitors set up a personal eating plan and track activity and eating levels, with recommendations for serving sizes, daily requirements, and eating plans to keep kids healthy.

National Eating Disorders Association (NEDA)

603 Stewart Street, Suite 803

Seattle, WA 98101

(800) 931-2237

Web site: http://www.edap.org

NEDA is the largest nonprofit organization that works to prevent eating disorders and to help people who are suffering from them.

National Institute of Mental Health (NIMH)

6001 Executive Boulevard, Room 8184, MSC 9663

Bethesda, MD 20892-9663

(866) 615-6464

Web site: http://www.nimh.nih.gov

The NIMH helps people learn about all aspects of mental health, including eating disorders.

Slow Food USA

20 Jay Street, #313

Brooklyn, NY 11201

(718) 260-8000

Web site: http://www.slowfoodusa.org

The Slow Food movement has many informal chapters in countries around the world. The movement encourages people to eat mindfully and enjoy local and seasonal food.

Web Sites

Due to the changing nature of Internet links, Rosen Publishing has developed an online list of Web sites related to the subject of this book. This site is updated regularly. Please use this link to access the list:

http://www. rosenlinks.com/idf/fake

FOR FURTHER READING

Cobb, Vicki. *Junk Food* (Where's the Science Here?). Minneapolis, MN: Millbrook Press, 2006.

Compart, Pamela J., and Dana Laake. *The Kid-Friendly ADHD & Autism Cookbook: The Ultimate Guide to the Gluten-Free, Casein-Free Diet*. Beverly, MA: Fair Winds Press, 2006.

Gilbert, Sara. *The Story of McDonald's*. Mankato, MN: Creative Education, 2009.

Harmon, Daniel E. *Obesity* (Coping in a Changing World). New York, NY: Rosen Publishing Group, 2007.

Johanson, Paula. *Processed Food* (What's in Your Food? Recipe for Disaster). New York, NY: Rosen Publishing Group, 2008.

Levin, Judith. *Frequently Asked Questions About Diabetes* (FAQ: Teen Life). New York, NY: Rosen Publishing Group, 2007.

Pollan, Michael. *Food Rules: An Eater's Manual*. New York, NY: Penguin, 2009.

Schlossen, Eric, and Charles Wilson. *Chew on This: Everything You Don't Want to Know About Fast Food*. Boston, MA: Houghton-Mifflin, 2006.

Smith, Alisa, and J. B. MacKinnon. *The 100-Mile Diet: A Year of Local Eating*. Toronto, ON, Canada: Random House, 2007.

Watson, Stephanie. *Binge Eating* (Danger Zone: Dieting and Eating Disorders). New York, NY: Rosen Publishing Group, 2007.

Watson, Stephanie. *Fast Food* (What's in Your Food? Recipe for Disaster). New York, NY: Rosen Publishing Group, 2008.

Ziczenko, David, and Matt Goulding. *Eat This, Not That! For Kids! Thousands of Simple Food Swaps That Can Save Your Child from Obesity*. Emmaus, PA: Rodale, 2008.

BIBLIOGRAPHY

Brandeis University. "New Fat, Same Old Problem with an Added Twist? Replacement for Trans Fat Raises Blood Sugar in Humans." ScienceDaily, January 18, 2007. Retrieved May 2, 2010 (http://www.sciencedaily.com/releases/2007/01/070116131545.htm).

Brooks, Megan. "Plasticizer May Be Tied to Boys' Breast Enlargement." Reuters, December 14, 2009. Retrieved May 20, 2010 (http://www.reuters.com/article/idUSTRE5BD39920091214).

Caughlan, Goldie. "TSP in Cheerios." PCC Natural Markets, June 2002. Retrieved May 11, 2010 (http://www.pccnaturalmarkets.com/sc/0206/goldies.html).

Deville, Nancy. *Death by Supermarket: The Fattening, Dumbing Down, and Poisoning of America.* Fort Lee, NJ: Barricade Books, 2007.

Ebert, Andy G. "Phosphates Uses in Foods." International Food Additives Council, 2007. Retrieved May 19, 2010 (http://www.foodadditives.org/phosphates/phosphates_used_in_food.html).

Ettlinger, Steve. *Twinkie, Deconstructed: My Journey to Discover How the Ingredients Found in Processed Foods Are Grown, Mined (Yes, Mined), and Manipulated into What America Eats.* New York, NY: Hudson Street Press, 2007.

Guyol, Gracelyn. *Healing Depression & Bipolar Disorder Without Drugs: Inspiring Stories of Restoring Mental Health Through Natural Therapies.* New York, NY: Walker & Company, 2006.

Kennedy, Robert F., Jr. *Crimes Against Nature: How George W. Bush and His Corporate Pals Are Plundering the Country and Hijacking Our Democracy.* New York, NY: HarperCollins, 2004.

Klein, Sarah, and Caroline Smith DeWaal. *Dirty Dining.* Washington, DC: Center for Science in the Public Interest, 2008.

Leiff, Cabraser, Heimann, & Bernstein, LLP. "New York Woman Files Suit Charging Butter Flavoring Chemical Diacetyl Led to Serious Lung Injury." Retrieved April 10, 2010 (http://www.butterflavoringlunginjury.com).

Mansbridge, Bruce. *The Complete Idiot's Guide to Conquering Obsessive-Compulsive Behavior.* New York, NY: Alpha Books, 2009.

Marler, Bill. "About Reactive Arthritis." About.com. Retrieved April 10, 2010 (http://www.about-reactive-arthritis.com).

Nestle, Marion. *Food Politics: How the Food Industry Influences Nutrition and Health.* Berkeley, CA: University of California Press, 2003.

Nestle, Marion. *What to Eat.* New York, NY: North Point Press, 2006.

Patel, Raj. "Down on the Clown." April 9, 2010. Retrieved May 20, 2010 (http://rajpatel.org).

Pfeiffer, Dale Allen. *Eating Fossil Fuels: Oil, Food and the Coming Crisis in Agriculture.* Gabriola Island, BC, Canada: New Society Publishers, 2006.

Pollan, Michael. *Food Rules: An Eater's Manual.* New York, NY: Penguin, 2009.

Pollan, Michael. *The Omnivore's Dilemma: A Natural History of Four Meals.* New York, NY: Penguin, 2006.

Smith, Rick, Bruce Lourie, and Sarah Dopp. *Slow Death by Rubber Duck: How the Toxic Chemistry of Everyday Life Affects Our Health.* Toronto, ON: Knopf, 2009.

Taylor, Paul. "Small Doses." *Globe and Mail,* April 30, 2010, p. L1.

United Nations Food and Agriculture Organization. "Carnauba Wax Data Sheet." Retrieved April 10, 2010 (http://www.fao.org/ag/agn/jecfa-additives/specs/Monograph1/Additive-109.pdf).

INDEX

About the Author

For twenty years, Paula Johanson has worked as a writer, teacher, and editor. She operated an organic-method market garden for fifteen years, selling produce and wool at farmers' markets. She has worked as a short-order cook and a sushi chef. Her nonfiction books on science and health topics include *Jobs in Sustainable Agriculture*, *Processed Food*, *Breast Cancer Prevention*, *Frequently Asked Questions About Testicular Cancer*, and *Making Good Choices About Fair Trade*. An accredited teacher, she has written and edited curriculum educational materials for the Alberta Distance Learning Centre and eTraffic Solutions.

Photo Credits

Cover (middle) Brand X Pictures/Thinkstock; cover (bottom), chapter openers, book art, pp. 14–15 Shutterstock; cover (top left), back cover, pp. 1, 4–5 © www. istockphoto.com/Sharon Dominick; p. 5 Robert Sullivan/AFP/Getty Images; p. 8 Eric Futran-Chefshots/FoodPix/Getty Images; p. 9 Francois Nascimbeni/AFP/Getty Images; p. 12 www.istockphoto.com/Thinkstock; p. 17 Hemera Technologies/ AbleStock.com/Thinkstock; p. 18 3D4Medical.com/Getty Images; p. 21 Science Photo Library/Custom Medical Stock Photo; p. 25 Kallista Images/Getty Images; p. 27 Aaron Haupt/Photo Researchers; p. 29 Dan McCoy/Rainbow/Science Faction/ Getty Images; p. 31 Rita Maas/The Image Bank/Getty Images; p. 32 Jupiter Images/ Photos.com/Thinkstock; p. 35 ML Harris/Iconica/Getty Images; p. 36 © AP Photos.

Designer: Les Kanturek; Editor: Kathy Kuhtz Campbell;
Photo Researcher: Marty Levick